T0088815

Cowboy Songs
for Harmonica
by Glenn Weiser

Foreword by
Ranger Doug Green

Cover Illustration by Dave Collins

To access audio, visit:
www.HalLeonard.com/MyLibrary
Enter Code
4476-3081-1610-3115

ISBN 978-1-57424-352-9

"Well, there it goes again . . . Every night when we bed down, that confounded harmonica starts in."

Table of Contents

Foreword

A lonesome prairie, a starlit night, a crackling campfire, a lonely cowboy, and the haunting sound of a harmonica…it is a cinematic cliche, but as Glenn Weiser points out, not an inaccurate one — harmonicas were indeed integral to the creation of cowboy and western music in the great trail drives and the winning of the west.

Ahead of you in this folio is a collection of the best known and best loved cowboy folk songs arranged for the harmonica player, suitable for beginner or virtuoso. It will take you on a journey into the past, into one of the most colorful and fascinating chapters in the history of the United States. Enjoy your journey, and as you play, imagine that lonesome prairie, that starlit night, that crackling campfire…it's the cowboy way.

Ranger Doug
Riders in the Sky

Acknowledgements

I'd like to thank the people who helped this book on its way: Ron Middlebrook of Centerstream Publishing for bringing out the book, Ranger Doug Green, for writing the foreword, and harmonica scholars Pat and Missin and Winslow Xerxa, who provided me with many essential details of the harmonica's early history.

Also, I was assisted with harmonica-related questions by a number of official state historians and archivists: Marshall Trimble of Arizona, Larry Brown of Wyoming, Sarah Gilmor of Colorado, and others.

Lastly, In choosing the tempos and melodic variants of the songs here I relied heavily on the recordings of contemporary cowboy singers Don Edwards and Michael Martin Murphy. Here's a big tip of my Stetson to these fine artists for keeping the old Western ballads alive.

GW

Introduction

In American popular culture the harmonica is indelibly associated with the cowboy, playing his plaintive, warbling melodies to while away the evening hours after the herd had stopped for the night. With few options for entertainment along the trail other than poetry, dancing, and music, it's no wonder that hundreds of songs emerged from the Old West telling of the cowpuncher's life, the exploits of famous outlaws, and other aspects of frontier existence. They were first collected and published early in the last century by Jack Thorp, Carl Sandburg, and John Lomax, who as a boy heard the cowboys singing at night on the Chisholm Trail where it began at San Antonio. In this book, you'll find 27 of these traditional ballads arranged for the 10-hole diatonic harmonica. All songs include music notation, harmonica tablature, guitar chords, lyrics, and online audio files with acoustic guitar backing tracks. I've also added a chapter on the history of cowboy harmonica which recounts the research I undertook to establish that rather than being a Hollywood invention as has been contended, some trail hands did in fact play the instrument on the long cattle drives.

Technique-wise, the harmonica can be played in either of two ways: using the pucker method, the player can purse his/her lips to create a vertical oval opening with which he/she sounds one note at a time, or with tongue blocking, he/she can play a single notes with the right corner of his/her mouth and lift his tongue off and on the holes to the left to create a chord line below the melody. Harmonica scholar and author Winslow Xerxa noted in an email that nineteenth century harmonica instructional books taught tongue blocking (the harmonica was designed to be played this way), but also thought it likely that some self-taught players of the time used puckering. In the classic western movies and TV shows, though, the harmonica style usually heard is single-note pucker with tremolo, which is the technique of rapidly cupping and uncupping the hands around the harmonica to create a warbling effect, used with the long notes. On the online audio files, this is how I demonstrate the songs (I often add releasing grace note bends to the high blow reeds as well. This is done by beginning the note bent and letting it quickly pop up to normal pitch.) To see how tongue blocking works, see my most recent book, "Bluegrass and Old-Time Fiddle Tunes for Harmonica."

All the songs here are arranged for standard Richter-tuned 10-hole diatonic harmonica. Some of the high-pitched tunes in the keys of C and D will sound better on low-tuned models, which are an octave below the regular diatonics. In many cases, I have also come up with new chord lines for the songs, which I hope you like. Also, for anyone interested in learning the tunes in this book I offer private lessons on Skype/Facetime, and also webcam instruction in a wide variety of musical styles on harmonica, guitar, banjo, mandolin, ukulele, and electric bass. See my website, **CelticGuitarMusic.com**, for details.

Enjoy the music.

Glenn Wesier
Southwick, MA

In Search of the Cowboy Harmonica:
Some History

The story of the harmonica-totin' cowboy starts with the Civil War. After hostilities ceased in 1865, the State of Texas found itself cash poor, but cattle rich. The Confederate money in the state's coffers was worthless. But, in the absence of the cattlemen who had gone off to fight for the South, the population of Texas longhorns, which up to then had been hunted as game animals, had grown to 5 or 6 million. And most of them were unbranded.

Because the supply of pork in the North was needed to feed Union troops, the population's preference in meat there shifted to beef. This created such an enormous demand for cows that steers valued at $4 a head in Texas could fetch $40 in Chicago, Cincinnati, and other meat-packing centers. The problem was how to get them there.

The nation's railroads were still expanding, and the closest railheads to Texas at the time were in Kansas. Starting in 1866, cowboys drove herds averaging from 2000-3000 animals 10 to 15 miles a day over several hundred miles from the Rio Grande or San Antonio first to Abilene via the Chisolm Trail and later, Dodge City, Wichita, Denver, and other points as additional routes opened up. A typical crew consisted of the trail boss, the cook, the wrangler, who looked after the horses, and a dozen or so drovers. Given the threat of cattle rustlers and stampedes, the cowpokes typically carried pistols and rifles for protection. In the following decades, the hard and dangerous work of 40,000 cowpunchers, a work force of whites, Mexicans, and blacks, brought some 10 million longhorns to market. Consequently, Texas returned to solvency.

During the heyday of the long drives, accounts of life on the trail were published in magazines like Harpers. Those reports, along with the artwork of Frederick Remington and the travelling Wild West shows of Buffalo Bill Cody and others, branded the figure of the bronco busting, steer roping buckaroo-upright, tough, and self-reliant-onto the public's imagination. Charles Goodnight, who with Oliver Loving opened the Goodnight-Loving Trail and for whom the chuck wagon was named, saluted the character of the cowboy, writing that "I wish I could find words to express the trueness, the bravery, the hardihood, the sense of honor, the loyalty to their trust and to each other of the old trail hands."

The cattle drives were a major industry until about 1890. Then, the ranchers who owned land through which the trails passed began to fence in their spreads with barbed wire, which had been invented in 1874 and was a major improvement over wooden fences. That, with the advent of refrigeration in the 1880s and the extension of railroads further south, brought the era to a close.

With the cowboy established as an American folk hero, Hollywood was quick to produce westerns, which remained the most popular film genre until the 1960s. And in many old cowboy movies or TV reruns, you'll see or hear the mouth harp in a quiet moment (often played by LA studio ace Tommy Morgan), as when in the 1952 classic High Noon the outlaws are at the depot waiting for the train and one of them is playing the harmonica. Gene Autry and Roy Rogers also made films in which the instrument was featured. In the 1947 The Stranger from Ponca City, two of Autry's harmonica players, Smiley Burnette and Bill Russell, have a harmonica duel to one-up each other's skill. Thus the cowboy and the harmonica became forever associated. If the movies were to be believed, you'd think a member of every trail crew or gang of stagecoach robbers toted one.

But did they, really? When I began this project, I wanted to know what if any historical evidence existed for cowboys, gunslingers and other denizens of the Old West having played the harmonica. After all, why write a book based on a Hollywood

COWBOY HARMONICA: SOME HISTORY

myth? So before I had engraved the first note of music in this book, I went online and undertook some research.

In a 2105 post on the Facebook page of Denver's Mile High Harmonica Club, Manfed Wewers pens an informative piece, "The Harmonica in the Wild West." He provides plenty of useful details about the role of the instrument in old westerns and the Hohner company's production totals in the late 19th century. Wewers also mentions that, according to tradition, Billy the Kid, Wyatt Earp, and Frank James all played the instrument, and recounts the oft-repeated tale that James' life was saved by a harmonica in his left breast pocket when a bullet ricocheted off of it. But he concedes that these stories can't be verified. Wewers goes on to say "The harmonica, because of its size, cost and availability, would have accompanied those settlers, cowboys and entrepreneurs on their journeys. The settler would have played the harmonica for entertainment and at dances; the cowboy, to soothe a restless herd, or his restless spirit, or just to while away time by the campfire; and the entrepreneur, to demonstrate its capability before selling it."

What I found with this piece and others was that the writers simply assumed that many cowhands had played harmonica and touted that as fact while offering no evidence for the claim.

Similarly, Marshall Trimble, the state historian of Arizona, responded to a query that I sent to the official historians of several western states, saying, "Harmonicas came out in the 1850s and were popular during the Civil War. Cowboys, miners and anybody else in the post-war years could play one. I've heard Billy the Kid played one. I know he liked music. Cowboys on the long drives from Texas up to Kansas would most certainly carried one. A harmonica was a good way to kill loneliness. And you could carry one in your vest pocket. No other instrument excepting a mouth harp could be taken on a trail ride. A guitar wouldn't survive the elements, neither would a fiddle. A fiddle or guitar would be fine around the bunkhouse but not out in the elements."

How did he know this, though? Guy W Logsdon, author of "The Whorehouse Bells Were Ringing and Other Songs Cowboys Sing," had looked into the question of pickers on the trail and was largely dismissive, saying in his preface: "My research dispelled another romantic concept. There were few, if any musical instruments in the cow camps. Certainly there were few, if any guitars; it, along with the harmonica, became a twentieth-century adaption imposed on the cowboy. The introduction and distribution of the harmonica probably limited its availability during the trail driving years, primarily the years between 1867 and 1890. The fiddle was the instrument most often mentioned in cowboy literature. The banjo from music hall and minstrel tradition was second in popularity. In fact, cowboys needed no instruments. Like traditional singers from other regions, they usually sang unaccompanied."

Logsdon was correct about the guitar-it was not widely played in America until the turn of the 20th century, and yes, up to then the fiddle had been the nation's most popular instrument. As for the harmonica, though, he admits uncertainty as to its availability at the time. I knew who could clear that up, though.

Answering an email, British harmonica scholar Pat Missin wrote, "Harmonica production was a very work intensive process for most of the Old West era. They didn't become cheap and readily available until the 1870s… It's entirely possible that Billy the Kid, Wyatt Earp and Frank James played harp, but they wouldn't have been played on the Oregon Trail, or during the California Gold Rush.

"Mass production of the harmonica coincided neatly with the development of the U.S. rail network and the rise of companies like Sears Roebuck and Montgomery Ward. The harmonica's size and price made it a popular item in the general stores of rural towns. This is all in the last few decades of the Old West."

COWBOY HARMONICA: SOME HISTORY

Now at least I could figure that cowboys arriving in railhead towns with money to spend could have bought harmonicas at the general stores. And of the 40,000 men working the trails, it's likely that some of them did. Mail-order ads for the instrument in newspapers were also common at the time-the cowboy could have easily sent away for one during the off season.

For example, Larry K. Brown, a volunteer researcher at the Wyoming State Archives, combed through a database of that state's old newspapers and wrote to me that "during my research on your subject I found 273 ads/articles/items re "harmonica" that appear in Wyoming newspapers during the period of Dec. 10, 1868 through Dec. 31, 1890." That showed that the harmonica was not rare in the Old West, but it did not put one in the hands of a cowboy.

Searching further online, I came across a reference to a harmonica tooting cowboy, a black cowpuncher named Charlie Willis, composer of "Goodbye, Old Paint." In her book "Black Cowboys of the Old West: True, Sensational, and Little-Known Stories," author Tricia Martineau Wagner writes, "Every trail boss recognized that music was good for morale. A cowboy who could play the fiddle was especially popular. Perhaps Charlie's talent of playing various musical instruments was another reason for being hired on trail drives. Musical instruments that were brought along the trail included the harmonica, or mouth organ, the guitar, the banjo, the fiddle, and the Jew's Harp, which Charlie could play."

That was even better, but still it cited no contemporary sources.

I finally hit pay dirt when Sarah Gilmor, a reference librarian at the Stephen H. Hart Library & Research Center at History Colorado in Denver, sent me a scan of a page form the July 2nd, 1887 edition of The Rocky Mountain News, the paper of record there for 150 years.

In an article entitled "Annual Round-Up," an unnamed correspondent chronicles the cowboy's working day. After describing how the cowhands staked down the night horses in the evening, he writes, "This done there follows several hours of singing and music from that little instrument of which the cowboy is master-the mouth-organ or harmonica. Elsewhere the mouth-organ is a plaything for children, but those who have heard know that skilled cowboys can extract from it melody it is no flattery to call good music."

Even though this was written in the twilight of the Old West, it established as firmly as anything I was likely to find that at least some cowpunchers did indeed play the harmonica. And quite well, too.

With that, I reached the end of a trail that began in postbellum Texas and had taken me through Hollywood legend and then through debunked myth and finally to historical fact. Satisfied, I returned to completing this book.

So now let's play some authentic old cowboy songs on the mouth harp, just like the old trail hands did.

Betsy from Pike

This is a Gold Rush-era song written by John A. Stone to the
tune of the Irish song "The Old Orange Flute." Carl Sandburg
collected it and published it in his 1927 book *American Songbag*.

C-Harmonica   Traditional, Arr. G. Weiser

Billy The Kid

Born Henry McCarty, Billy the Kid (1859-1881) was an outlaw who
fought in New Mexico's Lincoln County War and is known to have
killed eight men. The song was collected by John and Alan Lomax
and published in thier 1934 book *American Ballads and Folk Songs.*

D-Harmonica

Traditional, Arr. G. Weiser

Bucking Bronco

Atrributed to the outlaw Belle Starr, this is a rare cowboy song from
the woman's point of view. The song was collected by John Lomax and
published in his 1910 book *Cowboy Songs and Other Frontier Ballads.*

D-Harmonica

Traditional, Arr. G. Weiser

Oh, Bury Me Not
On The Lone Prairie

Many cowboys songs were reworkings of sea shanties. This
was originally published in 1839 as "The Ocean Burial," and
began "O bury me not in the deep, deep sea." The version
here uses a different melody than the one collected by
John Lomax in *Cowboy Songs and Other Frontier Ballads*.

G-Harmonica

Traditional, Arr. G. Weiser

The Colorado Trail

This was collected and published by Carl Sandburg
in *American Songbag.* The trail branched off the main
Western Trail in Oklahoma and ran northwest to Colorado.

C-Harmonica

Traditional, Arr. G. Weiser

The Cowboys' Christmas Ball

This was originally a poem by Lawrence Chitterdon that was later set to music. It appears in *Cowboy Songs and other Frontier Ballads.* The Cowboy's Christmas Ball has been held annually in Anson, Texas since 1885.

G-Harmonica

Traditional, Arr. G. Weiser

The Cowboy's Life

This is a reworking of a American lumberjack ballad from the Northeast, "A Shanty Man's Life," which in turn came from an English sea shanty. It was collected by John Lomax and published in *Cowboy Songs and Other Frontier Ballads.*

C-Harmonica

Traditional, Arr. G. Weiser

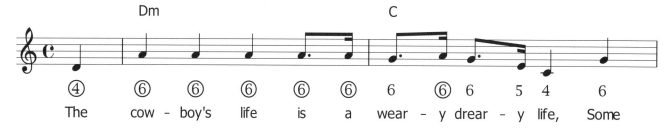

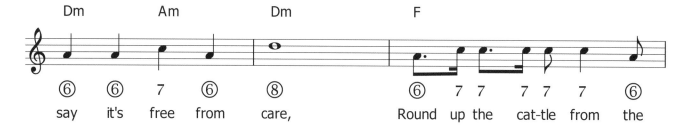

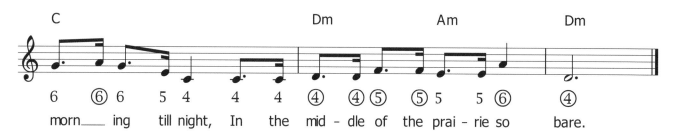

The cowboy's life is a weary, dreary life
Some say it's free from care
Round up the cattle from the morning till night
In the middle of the prairie so bare
Chorus

Half past four, the noisy cook will roar
"Whoop-a-whoop-a-hey!"
Slowly you will rise with sleepy feeling eyes
The sweet dreamy night has passed away!

The wolves and owls with their terrifying howls
Disturb us in our midnight dream
As we lie on our slickers on a cold, rainy night
Way over on the Pecos Stream
Chorus

Spring time sets in – double trouble will begin
The weather is so fierce and cold
Our clothes are wet and frozen to our neck
And the cattle we can scarcely hold
Chorus

A cowboy's life is a weary, dreary life
He's driven through the heat and cold
While the rich man's a-sleeping on his velvet couch
A-dreaming of his silver and his gold!
Chorus

The Cowboy's Ride

You'd never know it from the movies, but cowboys were fond of poetry and often recited verse in the evening while the herd was resting for the night. This song is an example of Old West lyricism, and was recored by John Lomax for the Library of Congress.

G-Harmonica

Traditional, Arr. G. Weiser

Oh, for a ride o'er the prai_ries free, on a fie – ry un – tamed steed, Where the cer – lews fly and the coy – otes cry, And the west – ern wind goes sweep – ing by, For my heart en–joys the speed.

Oh, for a ride o'er the prairies free,
On a fiery untamed steed,
Where the curlews fly and the coyotes cry
And the western wind goes sweeping by,
For my heart enjoys the speed.

With my left hand light on the bridle rein,
And the saddle girth pinched behind,
With the lariat tied at the pony's side
By my stout right arm that's true and tried,
We race with the whistling wind.

We're up and away in the morning light
As swift as a shooting star,
That suddenly flies across the sky,

And the wild birds whirl in quick surprise
At the cowboy's gay "Hurrah!"

As free as a bird o'er the rolling sea
We skim the pasture wide,
Like a seagull song we hurry along,
And the earth resounds with a galloping song
As we sail through the fragrant tide.

You can have your ride in the crowded town!
Give me the prairies free.
Where the curlews fly and the coyotes cry,
And the heart expands 'neath the open sky:
Oh, that's the ride for me!

Doney Gal

John Lomax collected this night-herding song from Mrs. Louise Henson of San
Antonio, Texas, and with his son Alan published it in their book *Our Singing Country*.
"Doney" is an Anglicization of the Spanish "dona," a term of respect for a woman.
John Lomax believed that this was among the last of the authenic cowboy songs.

G-Harmonica

Traditional, Arr. G. Weiser

Get Along, Little Dogies

Collected by John Lomax and published in his *Cowboy Songs and Other Frontier Ballads,* Roy Rogers sings this in his 1940 film *West of the Badlands.* It is derived from the Irish song, "Old Man Rocking the Cradle."

A-Harmonica

Traditional, Arr. G. Weiser

Goodbye, Old Paint

Composed by the black cowboy Charlie Willis, this was collected by John
Lomax and published in his *Cowboy Songs and Other Frontier Ballads*.

D-Harmonica

Charlie Willis, arr. G. Weiser

My foot in the stirrup, my pony won't stand
I'm leaving Cheyanne, I'm off for Montan'

Chorus:
Goodbye, old Paint, I'm a-leaving Cheyenne.
Goodbye, old Paint, I'm a-leaving Cheyenne.

Old Paint's a good pony, he paces when he can
Good bye, Little Annie, I'm off for Cheyanne
Chorus

Oh, hitch up your horses, and feed them some hay
And sit yourself by me so long as you stay
Chorus

My horses ain't hungry, they'll not eat your hay
My wagon is loaded and rolling away
Chorus

My foot in the stirrup, my reins in my hand,
Good morning, young lady, my horses won't stand
Chorus

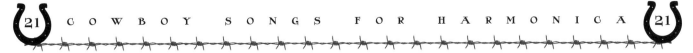

Green Grow The Lilacs

Based on the 17th century Scottish song, "Green Grows the Laurel", this newer version tells of an American soldier's love for a Mexican woman. Popular with the early Texas cowboys, western singer and film star Tex Ritter had a hit with it in 1945. A colorful legend holds that the Mexican word "gringo", meaning foreigner, derives from "green grow," the first two words of the song's title, but in fact the term dates back to at least 1797 and comes from the Spanish "griego," for "Greek."

C-Harmonica   Traditional, Arr. G. Weiser

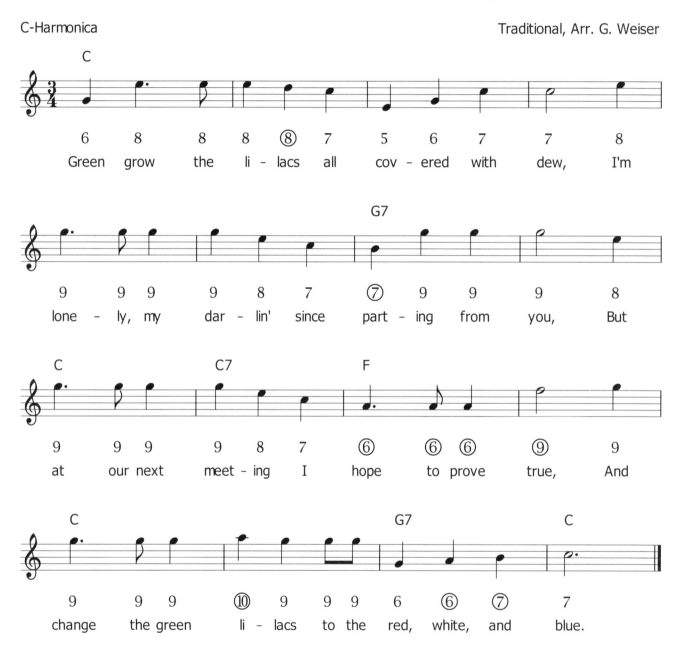

Home on the Range

The lyrics were originally written in the early 1870s in Kansas by Dr. Brewster
M. Higley in a poem entitled "My Western Home." The song was collected by
John Lomax and published in *Cowboy Songs and Other Frontier Ballads.*
It was a favorite of President Franklin D. Roosevelt in the 1930s.

G-Harmonica

Traditional, Arr. G. Weiser

I Ride An Old Paint

Collected by Carl Sanburg in *The American Songbag,*
the song was recorded in 1941 by Woody Guthrie.

G-Harmonica

Traditional, Arr. G. Weiser

Jesse James

Jesse James (1847-1882) was the most notorious of the Old West
outlaws, robbing banks, stagecoaches and trains with various gangs.
This song was written shortly after James' death. It was collected by
John Lomax and published in *Cowboy Songs and Other Frontier Ballads.*

G-Harmonica

Traditional, Arr. G. Weiser

The Lily of the West

This the American version of an Irish song. It was published in
1860. The version here is based on that of Peter, Paul, and Mary.

G-Harmonica

Traditional, Arr. G. Weiser

The Old Chisholm Trail

Collected and published by John Lomax in *Cowboy Songs and Other Frontier Ballads,*
this song dates back to the 1870s and was a favorite of the cowboys. The Chisholm
Trail was the first of the Old West cattle trails. The saying goes that for every mile
of the Chisholm Trail, there is a verse to the song. That's about 800 verses!
Note that on the third beat of measure 3 there is an optional chord change to Bm.

G-Harmonica

Traditional, Arr. G. Weiser

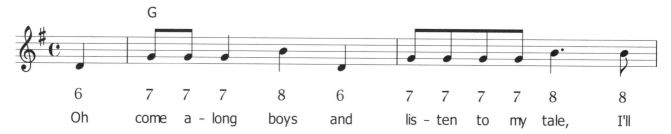

6   7   7   7   8   6   7   7   7   7   8   8

Oh   come a – long   boys   and   lis – ten   to   my   tale,   I'll

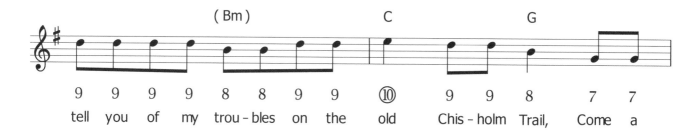

9   9   9   9   8   8   9   9   ⑩   9   9   8   7   7

tell   you   of   my   trou – bles   on   the   old   Chis – holm   Trail,   Come   a

⑧   8   ⑧   7   ⑥   6   7   7   8   9   8   ⑨

ti   yi   yip – pie   yip – pie   yea   yip – pie   yea,   Come   a

9   ⑩   9   ⑨   ⑧   ⑦   7

ti   yi   yip – pie   yip – pie   yea.

Red River Valley

This is among the most famous cowboy songs. It was collected by Carl Sanburg and published in *The American Songbag*. It concerns the Red River of the North, which flows northwards from Minnesota and North Dakota into Canada. Gene Autry sings it in his 1936 movie of the same name.

C-Harmonica

Traditional, Arr. G. Weiser

Rye Whiskey

Cowboys were usually not allowed to drink on the trail (falling off a horse was a common cause of death in the Old West), so when the buckaroos hit the railhead towns at the end of the cattle drives and got paid they often spent their money like sailors on liquor. John Lomax published a version of this song in 1910 under the title of "Jack of Diamonds," and Tex Ritter had a hit with it in 1933 for Columbia. The version here is based on the singing of Pete Seeger.

G-Harmonica

Traditional, Arr. G. Weiser

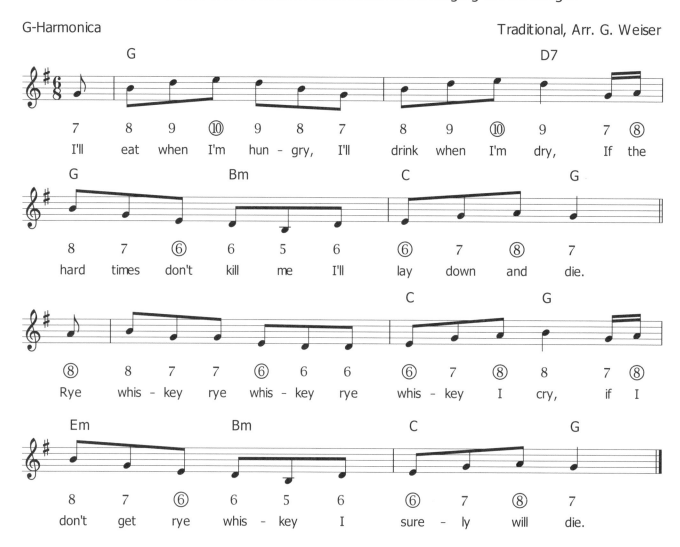

7 8 9 ⑩ 9 8 7   8 9 ⑩ 9   7 ⑧
I'll eat when I'm hun - gry, I'll drink when I'm dry, If the

8 7 ⑥ 6 5 6   ⑥ 7 ⑧ 7
hard times don't kill me I'll lay down and die.

⑧ 8 7 7 ⑥ 6 6   ⑥ 7 ⑧ 8   7 ⑧
Rye whis – key rye whis – key rye whis – key I cry, if I

8 7 ⑥ 6 5 6   ⑥ 7 ⑧ 7
don't get rye whis – key I sure – ly will die.

"Fording a stream"

A young John Wayne in the center.

Sam Bass

Sam Bass (1851-1878) was a notorious Old West outlaw. After he and his gang robbed a Union Pacific gold train of $60,000 in 1877, he was hunted down and killed in a shootout with the Texas Rangers. The song was collected by John Lomax and published in *Cowboy Songs and Other Frontier Ballads*. This version comes from the singing of John's son Alan.

D-Harmonica

Traditional, Arr. G. Weiser

3   4   4   4   4   4   5   4   ④   ④   ④   ④   4   ④

Sam   Bass was born   in   In – di an-a,   It   was   his   na – tive home,   And

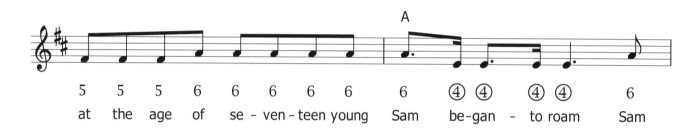

5   5   5   6   6   6   6   6   6   ④   ④   ④   ④   6

at   the   age   of   se – ven-teen young   Sam   be-gan – to roam   Sam

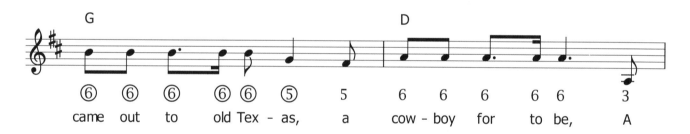

⑥   ⑥   ⑥   ⑥ ⑥   ⑤   5   6   6   6   6 6   3

came   out   to   old Tex – as,   a   cow – boy   for   to be,   A

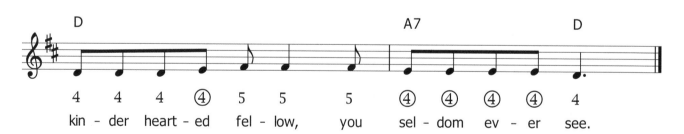

4   4   4   ④   5   5   5   ④   ④   ④   ④   4

kin – der heart – ed   fel – low,   you   sel – dom   ev – er   see.

Shenandoah

This beautiful early 19th century song tells of a French fur trader who falls in love with the daughter of the Algonquin cheif Shenandoah. W. B. Whall collected and published in his 1910 book *Ships, Sea Songs, and Shanties.*

D-Harmonica

Traditional, Arr. G. Weiser

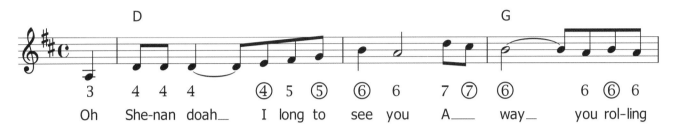

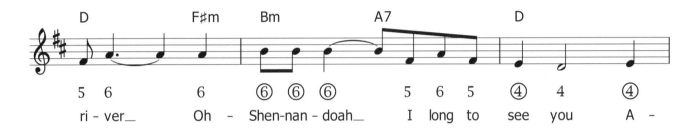

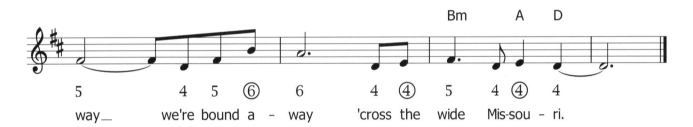

Oh Shenandoah, I long to see you,
Away you rolling river.
Oh Shenandoah, I long to see you,
Away, I'm bound away 'cross the wide Missouri.

Oh Shenandoah, I love your daughter,
Away, you rolling river.
For her I'd cross your roaming waters,
Away, I'm bound away cross the wide Missouri.

'Tis seven years since last I've seen you,
Away, you rolling river.
Tis seven years since last I've seen you,
Away, we're bound away cross the wide Missouri.

Oh Shenandoah, I long to hear you,
Away you rolling river.
Oh Shenandoah, I long to hear you,
Away, I'm bound away 'cross the wide Missouri.

The Strawberry Roan

The bronco buster broke in wild horses so they could work cattle drives. This song, written by California cowboy Curly Fletcher in 1915, concerns a red horse who shows a cowboy who's boss.

C-Harmonica

Traditional, Arr. G. Weiser

The Streets of Laredo

This is derived from an earlier Irish song, "The Unfortunate Rake".
It was collected by John Lomax and published in *Cowboy Songs and Other Frontier Ballads* under the title, "The Cowboy's Lament."

G-Harmonica

Traditional, Arr. G. Weiser

The Texas Cowboy

This was collected by John Lomax and published
in *Cowboy Songs and Other Frontier Ballads.*
A.J. Stinson was an early cattle baron in Arizona.

D-Harmonica

Traditional, Arr. G. Weiser

Oh, I'm a Tex - as cow-boy so far a - way from home, If
I get back to Tex - as I nev - er more shall roam, Mon -
tan - a is too cold for me, the win - ters are too long, Be -

fore the round - ups do be - gin our mon - ey is all gone.

Utah Carol

Stampedes were a deadly occupational hazard for the cowboy. This
song of heroism in such a situation was collected by John Lomax
and published in *Cowboy Songs and Other Frontier Ballads.*

C-Harmonica

Traditional, arr. G. Weiser

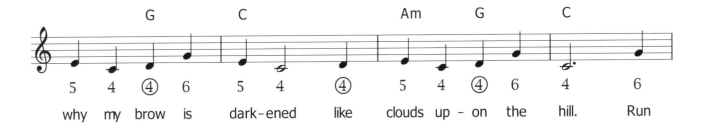

When The Work's All Done This Fall

Like "Utah Carroll," this tells of a cowboy who is killed in a stampede. It was first published in Miles City, Montana as a poem by D.J. O'Malley in the Oct. 6, 1893 edition of the *Stock-Growers Journal*. Seventeen years later the song was collected by John Lomax and published in *Cowboy Songs and Other Frontier Ballads*. Cowboy singer Carl T. Sprague recorded a famous version of it in 1925.

C-Harmonica

D. J. O'Malley, Arr. G. Weiser

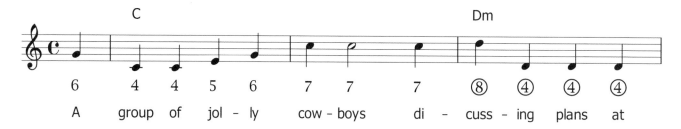

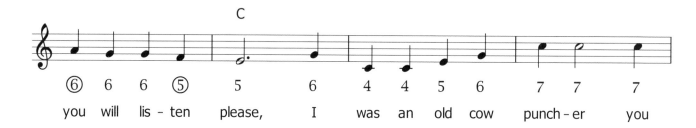

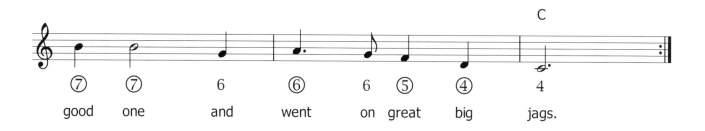

The Zebra Dunn

This story of tables turned was collected by Jack Thorp,
the first cowboy song gatherer, in 1890 and later
published in *Cowboy Songs and Other Frontier Ballads*.
The melody seems to be a variant of "Betsy from Pike."
This song should be played with a swing eighth feel.

C-Harmonica

Traditional, arr. G. Weiser

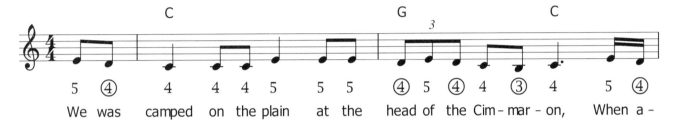

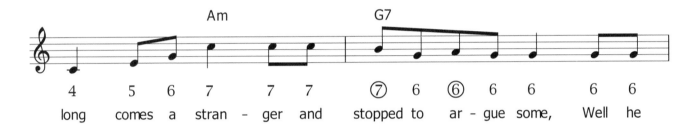

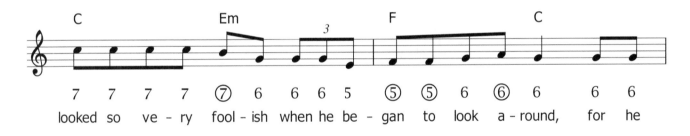

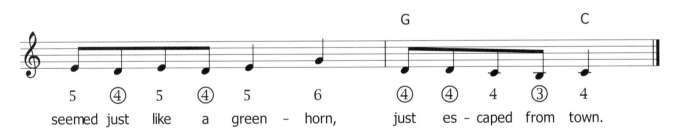

Additional Lyrics

BETSY FROM PIKE

Did you ever hear tell of Sweet Betsy from Pike,
Who crossed the wide mountains
    with her lover Ike,
And two yoke of cattle, a large yellow dog,
A tall Shanghai rooster, and a one-spotted hog.
Singing too-ra-li-oo-ra-li-oo-ra-li-ay.

They swam the wide rivers and
    crossed the tall peaks,
And camped on the prairie for weeks upon weeks.
Starvation and cholera, hard work and slaughter--
They reached California 'spite of hell
    and high water.
Singing too-ra-li-oo-ra-li-oo-ra-li-ay

One evening quite early they camped
    on the Platte,
'Twas near by the road on a green shady flat.
Betsy, sore-footed, lay down to repose--
With wonder Ike gazed on that Pike County rose.
Singing too-ra-li-oo-ra-li-oo-ra-li-ay

The Injuns came down in a thundering horde,
And Betsy was scared they would
    scalp her adored.
So under the wagon-bed Betsy did crawl
And she fought off the Injuns
    with musket and ball.
Singing too-ra-li-oo-ra-li-oo-ra-li-ay

The wagon broke down with a terrible crash,
And out on the prairie rolled all sorts of trash.
A few little baby-clothes, done up with care,
Looked rather suspicious, but all on the square.
Singing too-ra-li-oo-ra-li-oo-ra-li-ay

They stopped at Salt Lake to inquire of the way,
When Brigham declared that Sweet Betsy
    should stay.
Betsy got frightened and ran like a deer,
While Brigham stood pawing the ground
    like a steer.
Singing too-ra-li-oo-ra-li-oo-ra-li-ay

The alkali desert was burning and bare,
And Isaac's soul shrank from the death
    that lurked there.
"Dear old Pike County, I'll go back to you"--
Says Betsy, "You'll go by yourself if you do!"
Singing too-ra-li-oo-ra-li-oo-ra-li-ay

They soon reached the desert,
    where Betsy gave out,
And down in the sand she lay rolling about.
Ike in great wonder looked on in surprise,
Saying, "Betsy, get up,
    you'll get sand in your eyes."
Singing too-ra-li-oo-ra-li-oo-ra-li-ay

Sweet Betsy got up in a great deal of pain.
She declared she'd go back to Pike County again.
Ike gave a sigh, and they fondly embraced,
And they traveled along
    with his arm round her waist.
Singing too-ra-li-oo-ra-li-oo-ra-li-ay

The Shanghai ran off, and the cattle all died,
That morning the last piece of bacon was fried.
Ike got discouraged, Betsy got mad,
The dog drooped his tail
    and looked wonderfully sad.
Singing too-ra-li-oo-ra-li-oo-ra-li-ay

They suddenly stopped on a very high hill,
With wonder looked down upon old Placerville.
Ike said to Betsy, as he cast his eyes down,
"Sweet Betsy, my darling,
    we've got to Hangtown."
Singing too-ra-li-oo-ra-li-oo-ra-li-ay

Long Ike and Sweet Betsy attended a dance.
Ike wore a pair of his Pike County pants.
Betsy was covered with ribbons and rings.
Says Ike, "You're an angel,
    but where is your wings?"
Singing too-ra-li-oo-ra-li-oo-ra-li-ay

BETSY FROM PIKE (continued)

A miner said, "Betsy, will you dance with me?"
"I will that, old hoss, if you don't make too free.
Don't dance me hard, do you want to know why?
Doggone you, I'm chock-full of strong alkali."
Singing too-ra-li-oo-ra-li-oo-ra-li-ay

This Pike County couple got married, of course,
But Ike became jealous, and obtained a divorce.
Betsy, well-satisfied, said with a shout,
"Goodbye, you big lummox,
    I'm glad you backed out!"
Singing too-ra-li-oo-ra-li-oo-ra-li-ay

BILLY THE KID

I'll tell you the story of Billy the Kid
I'll sing of the desperate deeds that he did
Way out in New Mexico long, long ago
When a man's only chance was his own forty-four

When Billy the Kid was a very young lad
In old Silver City he went to the bad
Way out in the West with a gun in his hand
At the age of twelve years, he killed his first man

Fair Mexican maidens play guitars and sing
A song about Billy, their boy bandit king
Who ere his young man-hood
    had reached its sad end
Had a notch on his pistol for twenty-one men

'Twas on the same night, when poor Billy died
He said to his friends, 'I am not satisfied
Twenty-one men I have put bullets through
Sheriff Pat Garrett must make twenty-two'

Now this is how Billy the Kid met his fate
The bright moon was shining, the hour was late
Shot down by Pat Garrett,
    who once was his friend
The young outlaw's life had now come to its end

There's many a man with a face fine and fair
Who starts out in life with a chance to be square
But just like poor Billy, he wanders astray
And loses his life in the very same way

BUCKING BRONCO

My love is a rider, wild broncos he breaks
But he's promised to quit it all just for my sake
One foot he ties up and the saddle puts on
With a swing and a jump he is mounted and gone

The first time I saw him was early one spring
He was riding a bronco, a high-headed thing
He tipped me a wink as he gaily did go
For he wished me to look at his bucking bronco

The next time I saw him was late in the fall
He was swinging the ladies at Tomlinson's hall
We laughed and we talked
    as we danced to and fro
He promised never to ride on another bronco

He made me a present, among them a ring
But that which I gave him was a far better thing
'Twas a young maiden's heart,
    and I want you to know
He won it while riding his bucking bronco

Come all you young maidens, where'er you reside
Beware of the cowboy who swings the rawhide
He'll court you and then he will leave you and go
Up the trail in the spring on his bucking bronco

BURY ME NOT ON THE LONE PRAIRIE

"O bury me not on the lone prairie."
These words came low and mournfully
From the pallid lips of the youth who lay
On his dying bed at the close of day.

He had wasted and pined 'til o'er his brow
Death's shades were slowly gathering now
He thought of home and loved ones nigh,
As the cowboys gathered to see him die.

"O bury me not on the lone prairie
Where coyotes howl and the wind blows free
In a narrow grave just six by three—
O bury me not on the lone prairie"

"It matters not, I've been told,
Where the body lies when the heart grows cold
Yet grant, o grant, this wish to me
O bury me not on the lone prairie."

"I've always wished to be laid when I died
In a little churchyard on the green hillside
By my father's grave, there let me be,
O bury me not on the lone prairie."

"I wish to lie where a mother's prayer
And a sister's tear will mingle there.
Where friends can come and weep o'er me.
O bury me not on the lone prairie."

COLORADO TRAIL

Eyes like the morning star, cheeks like the rose,
Laura was a pretty girl, everybody knows,

Weep, all ye little rains, wail winds, wail,
All along, all along the Colorado Trail.

Laura was a laughing girl, joyful all the day.
Laura was my darling girl, now she's gone away.

Weep, all ye little rains, wail winds, wail,
All along, all along the Colorado Trail.

Sixteen years she graced the earth,
    and all life was good,
Now my life lies buried beneath a cross of wood,

Weep, all ye little rains, wail winds, wail,
All along, all along the Colorado Trail.

Ride all the lonely night, ride all the day,
Keep the herd a-rollin' on, rollin' on its way,

Weep, all ye little rains, wail winds, wail,
All along, all along the Colorado Trail.

Black is the stormy night, dark is the sky,
Wish I'd stayed in Abilene,
    nice and warm and dry,

Weep, all ye little rains, wail winds, wail,
All along, all along the Colorado Trail.

THE COWBOYS' CHRISTMAS BALL

Way out in West Texas,
    where the Clear Fork's waters flow,
Where the cattle are a-browsin'
    and the Spanish ponies grow;
Where the northers come a-whistlin'
    from beyond the Neutral Strip;
And the prairie dogs are sneezin',
    as though they had the grippe;
Where the coyotes come a-howlin'
    round the ranches after dark,
And the mockin' birds are singin'
    to the lovely medder lark;
Where the 'possum and the badger
    and the rattlesnakes abound,
And the monstrous stars are winkin'
    o'er a wilderness profound;
Where lonesome, tawny prairies
    melt into airy streams,
While the Double Mountains
    slumber in heavenly kinds of dreams;
Where the antelope are grazin'
    and the lonely plovers call,--
It was there that I attended
    the Cowboy's Christmas Ball.

The town was Anson City,
    old Jones' county seat,
Where they raised Polled Angus cattle
    and waving whiskered wheat;
Where the air is soft and balmy
    and dry and full of health,
Where the prairies is explodin'
    with agricultural wealth;
Where they print the _Texas Western_,
    that Hec McCann supplies
With news and yarns and stories,
    of most amazing size;
Where Frank Smith "pulls the badger"
    on knowing tenderfeet,
And Democracy's triumphant
    and mighty hard to beat;
Where lives that good old hunter,
    John Milsap, from Lamar,
Who used to be the sheriff
    "back east in Paris, sah"!

'Twas there, I say, at Anson
    with the lovely Widder Wall,
That I went to that reception,
    the Cowboy's Christmas Ball.
The boys had left the ranches
    and come to town in piles;
The ladies, kinder scatterin',
    had gathered in for miles.
And yet the place was crowded,
    as I remember well,
'Twas gave on this occasion
    at the Morning Star Hotel.
The music was a fiddle
    and a lively tambourine,
And a viol came imported,
    by the stage from Abilene.
The room was togged out gorgeous--
    with mistletoe and shawls,
And the candles flickered festious,
    around the airy walls.
The wimmen folks looked lovely--
    the boys looked kinder treed,
Till the leader commenced yelling,
    "Whoa, fellers, let's stampede,"
And the music started sighing
    and a-wailing through the hall
As a kind of introduction
    to the Cowboy's Christmas Ball.

The leader was a feller that came
    from Swenson's ranch,--
They called him Windy Billy
    from Little Deadman's Branch.
His rig was kinder keerless,--
    big spurs and high heeled boots;
He had the reputation
    that comes when fellers shoots.
His voice was like the bugle
    upon the mountain height;
His feet were animated,
    and a mighty movin' sight,
When he commenced to holler,
    "Now fellers, shake your pen!
Lock horns ter all them heifers
    and rustle them like men;

Saloot yer lovely critters;
  neow swing and let 'em go;
Climb the grapevine round 'em;
  neow all hands do-ce-do!
You maverick, jine the round-up,--
  jes skip the waterfall,"
Huh! hit was getting active,
  the Cowboy's Christmas Ball.

The boys was tolerable skittish,
  the ladies powerful neat,
That old bass viol's music
  just got there with both feet!
That wailin', frisky fiddle,
  I never shall forget;
And Windy kept a-singin'--
  I think I hear him yet--
"Oh, X's, chase yer squirrels,
  and cut 'em to our side;
Spur Treadwell to the center,
  with Cross P Charley's bride,
Doc Hollis down the center,
  and twine the ladies' chain,
Van Andrews, pen the fillies
  in big T Diamond's train.
All pull your freight together,
  neow swallow fork and change;
Big Boston, lead the trail herd
  through little Pitchfork's range.

Purr round yer gentle pussies,
  neow rope and balance all!"
Huh! Hit were gettin' active--
  the Cowboy's Christmas Ball.

The dust riz fast and furious;
  we all jes galloped round,
Till the scenery got so giddy
  that T Bar Dick was downed.
We buckled to our partners
  and told 'em to hold on,
Then shook our hoofs like lightning
  until the early dawn.
Don't tell me 'bout cotillions,
  or germans. No sir-ee!
That whirl at Anson City
  jes takes the cake with me.
I'm sick of lazy shufflin's,
  of them I've had my fill,
Give me a frontier break-down
  backed up by Windy Bill.
McAllister ain't nowhere,
  when Windy leads the show;
I've seen 'em both in harness
  and so I ought ter know.
Oh, Bill, I shan't forget yer,
  and I oftentimes recall
That lively gaited sworray--
  the Cowboy's Christmas Ball.

DONEY GAL

We're alone Doney gal in the wind and hail,
Got to drive them dogies down the trail,

We ride the range from sun to sun,
For a cowboy's work is never done,
We're up and gone at the break of day
Driving the dogies on their weary way

Chorus
Rain or shine, sleet or snow,
Me and my Doney gal we're bound to go
Rain or shine, sleet or snow,
Me and my Doney gal we're bound to go.

We're swimming rivers along the way,
And pushing for that north star day by day,
Rain or shine, sleet or snow,
Me and my Doney gal we're bound to go.
Chorus

Well a cowboy's life is a dreary thing,
For it's rope and brand and ride and sing,
Yes, night and day, and sleet and hail
We'll stay with the dogies on the trail.
Chorus

Tired and hungry, far from home
I'm just a poor cowboy bound to roam
Starless nights and lightning glare
Darkness and danger everywhere
Chorus

Round the campfires flickering glow,
We sing the songs from long, long ago,
we laugh at storms and sleet and snow
When we camp near San Antonio
Chorus

GET ALONG LITTLE DOGIES

As I was walking one morning for pleasure
I spied a young cowboy a- riding along
His hat was thrown back
        and his spurs were a-jingling
And as he approached he was singing this song

Chorus:
Whoopee ti yi yo, git along little dogies
It's your misfortune and none of my own
Whoopie ti yi yo, git along little dogies
You know that Wyoming will be your new home

Early in the springtime we round up the dogies
Mark 'em and brand 'em and bob off their tails
Round up the horses, load up the chuck wagon
Then throw the little dogies out on the long trail
Chorus

Night comes on and we
        hold 'em on the bedground
The same little dogies that rolled on so slow
We roll up the herd and cut out the stray ones
Then roll the little dogies like never before
Chorus

Some boys go up the long trail for pleasure
But that's where they get it most awfully wrong
For you'll never know the trouble they give us
As we go drivin' them dogies along
Chorus

GREEN GROW THE LILACS

Green grow the lilacs, all covered with dew
I'm lonely, my darling, since parting from you
But at our next meeting I hope to prove true,
And change the green lilacs
    to the red, white, and blue.

Once I had a sweetheart but now I've got none,
Since she has left me, I care for no one,
Since she's gone and left me, contented I must be,
For she loves another one better than me.

I passed by her window both early and late
The look that she gave me, it made my heart ache,
The look that she gave me was painful to see,
For she loves another one better than me.

I wrote my loved one with red rosy lines,
She sent me an answer all twisted with twines,
Sayin', Keep your love letters
    and I will keep mine,
Just you write to your love and I'll write to mine.

Green grow the lilacs, all covered with dew
I'm lonely, my darling, since parting from you
But at our next meeting I hope to prove true,
And change the green lilacs
    to the red, white, and blue.

HOME ON THE RANGE

Oh, give me a home where the buffalo roam,
and the deer and the antelope play,
Where seldom is heard a discouraging word
And the skies are not cloudy all day.

Chorus
Home, home on the range,
Where the deer and the antelope play;
Where seldom is heard a discouraging word
And the skies are not cloudy all day.

Where the air is so pure, the zephyrs so free,
The breezes so balmy and light,
That I would not exchange my home on the range
For all of the cities so bright.
Chorus

The red man was pressed
    from this part of the West
He's likely no more to return,
To the banks of Red River where seldom if ever
Their flickering camp-fires burn.
Chorus

How often at night when the heavens are bright
With the light from the glittering stars
Have I stood here amazed and asked as I gazed
If their glory exceeds that of ours.
Chorus

Oh, I love these wild prairies where I roam
The curlew I love to hear scream,
And I love the white rocks and the antelope flocks
That graze on the mountain-tops green.
Chorus

Oh, give me a land
    where the bright diamond sand
Flows leisurely down the stream;
Where the graceful white swan goes gliding along
Like a maid in a heavenly dream.
Chorus

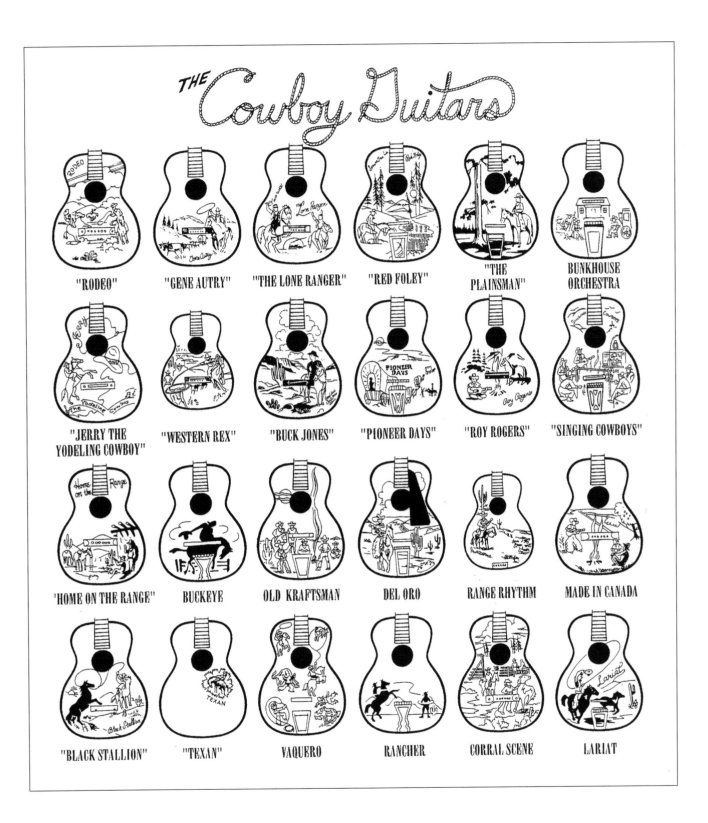

I RIDE AN OLD PAINT

I ride an old paint, I lead an old Dan,
I'm goin' to Montana to throw the houlian
They feed in the coulees, they water in the draw,
Tails are all matted and their backs are all raw

Chorus
Ride around, little doggies, ride around them slow,
They're fiery and snuffy and a-rarin' to go

Old Bill Jones had two daughters and a song,
One went to college, and the other went wrong
His wife got killed in a free-for-all fight,
Still he keeps singin' from mornin' till night
Chorus

I've worked in your town, worked on your farm,
And all I got to show is the muscle in my arm,
Blisters on my feet, and the callus on my hand,
And I'm a-goin' to Montana to throw the houlian
Chorus

Oh when I die, take my saddle from the wall
Put it on my pony, lead him out of his stall
Tie my bones to his back, turn our faces to the west
And we'll ride the prairies that we love the best
Chorus

JESSE JAMES

Jesse James was a lad who killed many a man
He robbed the Glendale train
He stole from the rich and he gave to the poor
He'd a hand and a heart and a brain

Chorus
Well Jesse had a wife to mourn for his life
Three children they were brave
Well that dirty little coward who shot Mr. Howard
And he laid poor Jesse in his grave

Well it was Robert Ford that dirty little coward
I wonder now how he feels
For he ate of Jesse's bread
    and he slept in Jesse's bed
And he laid poor Jesse in his grave
Chorus

Well now Jesse was a man a friend to the poor
He'd never rob a mother or a child
There never was a man with the law in his hand
That could take Jesse James when alive
Chorus

It was on a Saturday night
    the moon was shinin' bright
They robbed the Glendale train
And the people they did say o'er many miles away
It was those outlaws Frank and Jesse James
Chorus

Now Jesse went to rest
    with his hand upon his breast
The devil upon his knee
He was born one day in the County Clay
And he came from a solitary race
Chorus

Now the people held their breath
    when they heard of Jesse's death
They wondered how he'd ever come to fall
Robert Ford it was a fact he shot Jesse in the back
While Jesse hung a picture on a wall
Chorus

This song it was made by Billy Gashade
As soon as the new did arrive
There never was a man with the law in his hand
Who could take Jesse James when alive.
Chorus

LILY OF THE WEST

When first I came to Louisville,
    my fortune for to find,
I met a fair young maiden there,
    her beauty filled my mind.
Her rosy cheeks, her ruby lips,
    they gave my heart no rest.
The name she bore was Flora,
    the Lily of the West.

I courted lovely Flora,
    she promised ne'er to go.
But soon a tale was told to me
    that filled my heart with woe.
They said she meets another man
    who holds my love in jest.
And yet I trusted Flora,
    the Lily of the West.

'Way down in yonder shady grove,
    a man of low degree,
He spoke unto my Flora there
    and kissed her 'neath a tree.
The answers that she gave to him
    like arrows pierced my breast.
I was betrayed by Flora, the Lily of the West.

I stepped up to my rival,
    my dagger in my hand.
I seized him by the collar and
    I ordered him to stand.
All in my desperation
    I stabbed him in his breast.
I killed a man for Flora, the Lily of the West.

I had to stand my trial,
    I had to make my plea.
They placed me in a pris'ner's dock
    and then commenced on me.
Although she swore my life away,
    deprived me of my rest.
Still I love my faithless Flora, the Lily of the West.

RED RIVER VALLEY

From this valley they say you are going
We will miss your bright eyes and sweet smile
For they say you are taking the sunshine
That has brightened our pathways a while

Chorus:
Come and sit by my side, if you love me
Do not hasten to bid me adieu
Just remember the Red River Valley
And the cowboy who loved you so true

I've been thinking a long time, my darling
Of the sweet words you never would say
Now, alas, must my fond hopes all vanish?
For they say you are going away

Chorus

Do you think of the valley you're leaving?
O how lonely and how dreary it will be
Do you think of the kind hearts you're breaking?
And the pain you are causing to me
Chorus

They will bury me where you have wandered
Near the hills where the daffodils grow
When you're gone from the Red River Valley
For I can't live without you I know
Chorus

THE OLD CHISHOLM TRAIL

Well, come along boys and listen to my tale
I'll tell you of my troubles
 on the old Chisholm Trail
Come a-ti yi yippy, yippy yea, yippy yea
Come a-ti yi yippy, yippy yea.

I started up the trail October twenty-third
Started up the trail with the U-2 herd.
Come a-ti yi yippy, yippy yea, yippy yea
Come a-ti yi yippy, yippy yea.

On a ten-dollar horse and a forty-dollar saddle
Started out punchin' them long horn cattle
Come a-ti yi yippy, yippy yea, yippy yea
Come a-ti yi yippy, yippy yea.

I woke up one morning on the old Chisholm Trail
Rope in my hand and a cow by the tail
Come a-ti yi yippy, yippy yea, yippy yea
Come a-ti yi yippy, yippy yea.

With my seat in the saddle
 and my hand on the horn
I'm the best dang cowboy that was ever born
Come a-ti yi yippy, yippy yea, yippy yea
Come a-ti yi yippy, yippy yea.

It's cloudy in the west and lookin' like rain
And my danged old slicker's in the wagon again
Come a-ti yi yippy, yippy yea, yippy yea
Come a-ti yi yippy, yippy yea.

Goin' to the boss to get my money
Goin' back south to see my honey
Come a-ti yi yippy, yippy yea, yippy yea
Come a-ti yi yippy, yippy yea.

With my hand on the horn and my seat in the sky
I'll quit herding cows in the sweet by-and-by
Come a-ti yi yippy, yippy yea, yippy yea
Come a-ti yi yippy, yippy yea.

RYE WHISKEY

I'll eat when I'm hungry,
I'll drink when I'm dry,
If the hard times don't kill me,
I'll lay down and die.

(Chorus)
Rye whisky, rye whisky,
Rye whisky, l cry,
If I don't get rye whiskey,
I surely will die.

I'll tune up my fiddle,
And I'll rosin my bow,
I'll make myself welcome,
Wherever I go.

Beefsteak when I'm hungry,
Red liquor when I'm dry,
Greenbacks when I'm hard up,
And religion when I die.

Jack o' diamonds, jack o' diamonds,
I know you of old,
You've robbed my poor pockets
Of silver and gold.

Oh, whisky, you villain,
You've been my downfall,
You've kicked me, you've cuffed me,
But I love you for all.

You may boast of your knowledge
And brag of your sense,
'Twill all be forgotten
A hundred years hence.

My foot's in my stirrup,
My bridle's in my hand,
I'm leaving sweet Lillie,
The fairest in the land.

Tex Ritter.

SAM BASS

Sam Bass was born in Indiana,
    it was his native home,
And at the age of seventeen,
    young Sam began to roam.
Sam first came out to Texas a cowboy for to be-
A kinder-hearted fellow you seldom ever see.

Sam used to deal in race stock,
    one called the Denton mare;
He matched her in scrub races
    and took her to the fair.
Sam used to coin the money
    and spent it just as free,
He always drank good whiskey
    wherever he might be.

Sam left the Collins ranch
    in the merry month of May
With a herd of Texas cattle
    the Black Hills for to see,
Sold out in Custer City and then got on a spree-
A harder set of cowboys you seldom ever see.

On their way back to Texas
    they robbed the U.P. train,
And then split up in couples and started out again.
Joe Collins and his partner were overtaken soon,
With all their hard-earned money
    they had to meet their doom.
Sam made it back to Texas
    all right side up with care;
Rode into the town of Denton
    with all his friends to share.
Sam's life was short in Texas;
    three robberies did he do:
He robbed all the passenger, mail,
    and express cars too.

Sam had four companions-
    four bold and daring lads-
They were Richardson, Jackson,
    Joe Collins, and Old Dad;
Four more bold and daring cowboys
    the rangers never knew,
They whipped the Texas Rangers
    and ran the boys in blue.

Sam had another companion,
    called Arkansas for short,
Was shot by a Texas Ranger
    by the name of Thomas Floyd;
Oh, Tom is a big six-footer
    and thinks he's mighty fly,
But I can tell you his racket-
    he's a deadbeat on the sly.

Jim Murphy was arrested
    and then released on bail
He jumped his bond at Tyler
    and then took the train for Terrell;
But Mayor Jones had posted Jim
    and that was all a stall,
'Twas was only a plan to capture Sam
    before the coming fall.

Sam met his fate at Round Rock,
    July the twenty-first,
They pierced poor Sam with rifle balls
    and emptied out his purse,
Poor Sam he is a corpse and six foot under clay,
And Jackson's in the bushes trying to get away.

Jim bad borrowed Sam's good gold
    and didn't want to pay,
The only shot he saw was to give poor Sam away.
He sold out Sam and Barnes
    and left their friends to mourn
Oh, what a scorching Jim will get
    when Gabriel blows his horn.

And so he sold out Sam and Barnes
    and left their friends to mourn,
Oh, what a scorching Jim will get
    when Gabriel blows his horn.
Perhaps he's got to heaven,
    there's none of us can say
But if I'm right in my surmise
    he's gone the other way.

STRAWBERRY ROAN

I was layin' 'round town just a-passing my time,
Out of a job, not making a dime
When a feller steps up and he says, "I suppose
You're a bronc' bustin' man
    by the looks of your clothes."
"You guessed me right, and a good one," I claim,
"Do you happen to have any bad ones to tame?"
He says, "I've got one and a bad one to buck;
At throwin' bronc riders he's had lots of luck."

Chorus:
Well, it's oh, that strawberry roan,
Oh, that strawberry roan!
He says, "This old pony ain't never been rode,
And the man that gets on him
    is sure to get throwed."
Oh, that strawberry roan!

I gets all excited and I ask what he pays
To ride this old goat for a couple of days.
He offers a ten spot. I says, "I'm your man,
For the bronc never lived that I couldn't fan;
No, the bronc never lived,
    nor he never drew breath
That I couldn't ride
    till be starved plumb to death."
He says, "Get your saddle, I'll give you a chance."
We got in the buckboard and rode to the ranch.

Well, it's oh, that strawberry roan,
Oh, that strawberry roan!
We stayed until morning, and right after chuck
We goes out to see how that outlaw could buck.
Oh, that strawberry roan!

Well, down in the horse corral standing alone,
Was that old cavayo, old strawberry roan.
His legs were spavined, and he had pigeon toes,
Little pig eyes and a big Roman nose,
Little pin ears that were crimped at the tip,
With a big 44 branded 'cross his left hip;
He's ewe-necked and old, with a long lower jaw,
You can see with one eye he's a reg'lar outlaw.

Well, it's oh, that strawberry roan,
Oh, that strawberry roan!
He's ewe-necked and old, with a long lower jaw,
You can see with one eye he's a reg'lar outlaw.
Oh, that strawberry roan!

Well I puts on my spurs and I coils up my twine,
I piled my loop on him, I'm sure feeling fine.
I piled my loop on him, and well I knew then,
If I rode this old pony, I'd sure earn my ten,
I put the blinds on him, it sure was a fight,
Next comes my saddle, I screws her down tight
I gets in his middle and opens the blind,
I'm right in his middle to see him unwind
Well, it's oh, that strawberry roan,
Oh, that strawberry roan!
He lowered his old neck and I think he unwound
He seemed to quit living
    down there on the ground
Oh, that strawberry roan!

He went up towards the east and came down
towards the west,
To stay in his middle I'm doin' my best,
He's about the worst bucker I've seen on the range
He can turn on a nickel
    and give you some change.
He turns his old belly right up to the sun
He sure is one sun-fishin' son of a gun!
I'll tell you, no foolin', this pony can step,
But I'm still in his middle and buildin' a rep

Well, it's oh, that strawberry roan,
Oh, that strawberry roan!
He goes up on all fours
    and comes down on his side
I don't know what keeps him from losin' his hide
Oh, that strawberry roan!

STRAWBERRY ROAN (continued)

I loses my stirrup and also my hat,
I starts pulling leather, I'm blind as a bat;
With a big forward jump he goes up on high
Leaves me sittin' on nothin' way up in the sky
I turns over twice, and I comes back to earth
I lights in a-cussin' the day of his birth
I know there is ponies I'm unable to ride
Some are still living, they haven't all died.

Well, it's oh, that strawberry roan,
Oh, that strawberry roan!
I'll bet all my money the man ain't alive
That can stay with old strawberry
    when he makes his high dive.
Oh, that strawberry roan!

THE STREETS OF LAREDO

As I walked out in the streets of Laredo
As I walked out in Laredo one day
I saw a young cowboy all wrapped in white linen
All wrapped in white linen as cold as the clay

"I see by your outfit that you are a cowboy"
These words he did say as I boldly stepped by
"Come sit down beside me and hear my sad story
I am shot in the breast and I know I must die

"It was once in the saddle I used to go dashing
It was once in the saddle I used to go gay
But I first took to drinkin' and then to card playin'
Got shot in the breast and I am dying today

"Oh, beat the drum slowly and play the fife lowly
Play the dead march as you carry me along
Take me to the green valley,
    there lay the sod o'er me
For I'm a young cowboy
    and I know I've done wrong

"Get six jolly cowboys to carry my coffin
Get six pretty maidens to bear up my pall
Put bunches of roses all over my coffin
Put roses to deaden the sods as they fall

"Then swing your rope slowly
    and rattle your spurs lowly
And give a wild whoop as you carry me along
And in the grave throw me
    and roll the sod o'er me
For I'm a young cowboy
    and I know I've done wrong

"Go bring me a cup, a cup of cold water
To cool my parched lips," the cowboy then said
Before I returned his soul had departed
And gone to the round-up, the cowboy was dead

We beat the drum slowly and played the fife lowly
And bitterly wept as we bore him along
For we all loved our comrade,
    so brave, young, and handsome
We all loved our comrade
    although he'd done wrong

THE TEXAS COWBOY

Oh, I'm a Texas cowboy,
So far away from home,
If I get back to Texas
I never more shall roam.
Montana is too cold for me
And the winters are too long,
Before the round-ups do begin
Our money is all gone.

Take this old hen-skin bedding,
Too thin to keep me warm,
I nearly freeze to death, my boys.
Whenever there's a storm.
And take this old "tarpoleon,"
Too thin to shield my frame,
I got it down in Nebraska
A-dealin' a Monte game.

Now to win these fancy leggins
I'll have enough to do;
They cost me twenty dollars
The day that they were new.
I have an outfit on the Mussel Shell,
But that I'll never see,
Unless I get sent to represent
The Circle or D.T.

I've worked down in Nebraska
Where the grass grows ten feet high,
And the cattle are such rustlers
That they seldom ever die;
I've worked up in the sand hills
And down upon the Platte,
Where the cowboys are good fellows
And the cattle always fat;

I've traveled lots of country,
Nebraska's hills of sand,
Down through the Indian Nation,
And up the Rio Grande.
But the Bad Lands of Montana
Are the worst I ever seen,
The cowboys are all tenderfeet
And the dogies are too lean.

If you want to see some bad lands,
Go over on the Dry;
You will bog down in the coulees
Where the mountains reach the sky.
A tenderfoot to lead you
Who never knows the way,
You are playing in the best of luck
If you eat more than once a day.

Your grub is bread and bacon
And coffee black as ink;
The water is so full of alkali
It is hardly fit to drink.
They will wake you in the morning
Before the break of day,
And send you on a circle
A hundred miles away.

All along the Yellowstone
'Tis cold the year around;
You will surely get consumption
By sleeping on the ground.
Work in Montana
Is six months in the year;
When all your bills are settled
There is nothing left for beer.

Come all you Texas cowboys
And warning take from me,
And do not go to Montana
To spend your money free.
But stay at home in Texas
Where work lasts the year around,
And you will never catch consumption
By sleeping on the ground.

UTAH CAROL

And now my friends you've asked me
    what makes me sad and still
And why my brow is darkened
    like the clouds upon the hill
Run in your ponies closer
    and I'll tell to you my tale
Of Utah Carol my partner
    and his last ride on the trail

We rode the range together
    and rode it side by side
I loved him like a brother,
    and I wept when Utah died
We were rounding up one morning
    when work was almost done
When on his side the cattle started
    on a frightened run

Underneath the saddle
    that the boss's daughter rode
Utah that very morning
    had placed a bright red robe
So the saddle might ride easy
    for Lenore his little friend
And it was this red blanket
    that brought him to his end

The blanket was now dragging
    behind her on the ground
The frightened cattle saw it
    and charged it with a bound
Lenore then saw her danger
    and turned her pony's face
And leaning in the saddle
    tied the blanket to its place

But in leaning lost her balance,
    fell in front of that wild tide
"Lay still Lenore I'm coming"
    were the words that Utah cried
His faithful pony saw her
    and reached her in a bound
I thought he'd been successful,
    and raised her from the ground

But the weight upon the saddle
    had not been felt before
His backcinch snapped like thunder
    and he fell by Lenore
Picking up the blanket
    he swung it over his head
And started cross the prairie,
    "Lay still Lenore" he said

When he got the stampede turned
    and saved Lenore his friend
He turned to face the cattle
    and meet his fatal end
His six gun flashed like lightning,
    the report rang loud and clear
As the cattle rushed and killed him
    he dropped the leading steer

On his funeral morning I heard the preacher say
I hope we'll all meet Utah
    at the roundup far away
Then they wrapped him in a blanket
    that saved his little friend
And it was this red blanket
    that brought him to his end

WHEN THE WORK'S ALL DONE THIS FALL

A group of jolly cowboys,
　　discussing plans at ease.
Says one, "I'll tell you something, boys,
　　if you will listen, please
I am an old cow-puncher
　　and here I'm dressed in rags,
I used to be a tough one and go on great big jags.

CHORUS:
"After the round-ups are over
　　and after the shipping is done
I am going right straight home, boys,
　　ere all my money is gone
I have changed my ways, boys, no more will I fall;
And I am going home, boys,
　　when the work is done this fall.

"But I've got a home, boys,
　　a good one, you all know,
Although I have not seen it since long, long ago.
I'm going back to Dixie once more to see them all;
I'm going back to see my mother
　　when the work's all done this fall.

"When I left home, boys, my mother for me cried,
Begged me not to go, boys,
　　for me she would have died;
My mother's heart is breaking,
　　breaking for me, that's all,
And with God's help I'll see her
　　when the work's all done this fall."

This very night this cowboy
　　went out to stand his guard;
The night was dark and cloudy
　　and storming very hard;
The cattle they got frightened
　　and rushed in wild stampede,
The cowboy tried to head them,
　　riding at full speed.

While riding in the darkness
　　so loudly did he shout,
Trying his best to head them
　　and turn the herd about
His saddle horse did stumble and on him did fall
The poor boy won't see his mother
　　when the work's all done this fall.

His body was so mangled
　　the boys all thought him dead,
They picked him up so gently
　　and laid him on a bed;
He opened wide his blue eyes
　　and looking all around
He motioned to his comrades
　　to sit near him on the ground.

"Boys, send Mother my wages,
　　the wages I have earned,
For I'm afraid, boys, my last steer I have turned.
I'm going to a new range, I hear my Master's call,
And I'll not see my mother
　　when the work's all done this fall

"Fred, you take my saddle;
　　George, you take my bed;
Bill, you take my pistol after I am dead;
And think of me kindly
　　when you look upon them all,
For I'll not see my mother
　　when work is done this fall."

Poor Charlie was buried at sunrise,
　　no tombstone at his head,
Nothing but a little board; and this is what it said:
Charlie died at daybreak, he died from a fall,
And he'll not see his mother
　　when the work's all done this fall.

THE ZEBRA DUNN

We were camped on the plains
    at the head of the Cimarron
When along came a stranger
    and stopped to argue some.
He looked so very foolish
    when he began to look around,
We thought he was a greenhorn
    just escaped from town.

We asked if he had been to breakfast;
    he hadn't had a smear,
So we opened up the chuck-box
    and bade him have his share.
He took a cup of coffee
    and some biscuits and some beans,
And then began to talk and tell
    about foreign kings and queens,

About the Spanish war and fighting on the seas
With guns as big as steers
    and ramrods big as trees,
And about old Paul Jones,
    a mean, fighting son of a gun,
Who was the grittiest cuss that ever pulled a gun.

Such an educated feller
    his thoughts just came in herds,
He astonished all them cowboys
    with them jaw-breaking words.
He just kept on talking
    till he made the boys all sick,
And they began to look around
    just how to play a trick.

He said he had lost his job upon the Santa Fé
And was going across the plains to strike the 7-D.
He didn't say how come it,
    some trouble with the boss,
But said he'd like to borrow a nice fat saddle hoss.

This tickled all the boys to death,
    they laughed way down in their sleeves,
"We will lend you a horse
    just as fresh and fat as you please."
Shorty grabbed a lariat
    and roped the Zebra Dun

And turned him over to the stranger
    and waited for the fun.

Old Dunny was a rocky outlaw
    that had grown so awful wild
That he could paw the white out of the moon
    every jump for a mile.
Old Dunny stood right still,
    as if he didn't know,
Until he was saddled and ready for to go.

When the stranger hit the saddle,
    old Dunny quit the earth
And traveled right straight up
    for all that he was worth.
A-pitching and a-squealing,
    a-having wall-eyed fits,
His hind feet perpendicular,
    his front ones in the bits.

We could see the tops of the mountains
    under Dunny every jump,
But the stranger he was growed there
    just like the camel's hump;
The stranger sat upon him
    and curled his black mustache
Just like a summer boarder waiting for his hash.

He thumped him in the shoulders
    and spurred him when he whirled,
To show them flunky punchers
    that he was the wolf of the world.
When the stranger had dismounted
    once more upon the ground,
We knew he was a thoroughbred
    and not a gent from town;

The boss who was standing round
    watching of the show,
Walked right up to the stranger
    and told him he needn't go,--
"If you can use the lasso
    like you rode old Zebra Dun,
You are the man I've been looking for
    ever since the year one."

Oh, he could twirl the lariat
and he didn't do it slow,
He could catch them fore feet nine out of ten
for any kind of dough.
And when the herd stampeded
he was always on the spot
And set them to nothing, like the boiling of a pot.

There's one thing and a shore thing
I've learned since I've been born,
That every educated feller
ain't a plumb greenhorn.